JOHN
McCAIN
An American Life

GROSSET & DUNLAP
Published by the Penguin Group
Penguin Group (USA) Inc., 375 Hudson Street, New York, New York 10014, USA
Penguin Group (Canada), 90 Eglinton Avenue East, Suite 700,
Toronto, Ontario M4P 2Y3, Canada
(a division of Pearson Penguin Canada Inc.)
Penguin Books Ltd., 80 Strand, London WC2R 0RL, England
Penguin Group Ireland, 25 St. Stephen's Green, Dublin 2, Ireland
(a division of Penguin Books Ltd.)
Penguin Group (Australia), 250 Camberwell Road,
Camberwell, Victoria 3124, Australia
(a division of Pearson Australia Group Pty. Ltd.)
Penguin Books India Pvt. Ltd., 11 Community Centre, Panchsheel Park,
New Delhi—110 017, India
Penguin Group (NZ), 67 Apollo Drive, Rosedale, North Shore 0632, New Zealand
(a division of Pearson New Zealand Ltd.)
Penguin Books (South Africa) (Pty.) Ltd., 24 Sturdee Avenue,
Rosebank, Johannesburg 2196, South Africa

Penguin Books Ltd., Registered Offices:
80 Strand, London WC2R 0RL, England

Photo credits: cover and title page: © AP Photo/M. Spencer Green; pages 4-5: © AP Photo/LM
Otero; page 6: © AP Photo/Manuel Balce Ceneta; page 7: © AP Photo/Library of Congress;
page 8: © Associated Press; page 9: © Associated Press; page 10: © Terry Ashe/Time Life
Pictures/Getty Images; page 11: © AP Photo/Mary Ann Chastain; page 12: courtesy of the
McCain Campaign; page 13: © AP Photo/Gail Burton; pages 14-15: © AP Photo/Steve Helber;
page 15: © MPI/Getty Images; page 16: © Carrie Johnson/iStock; pages 16-17: © Malcolm
Romain/iStock; page 17: © iStock; page 18: © Hoang Dinh Nam/AFP/Getty Images; page 19:
© iStock; page 20: © Ronald S. Haeberle/Time Life Pictures/Getty Images; page 21: © Larry
Burrows/Time Life Pictures/Getty Images; pages 22-23: © Associated Press; page 24: © Hulton
Archive/Getty Images; page 25: © David Zaitz; page 27: © Associated Press; pages 28-29: ©
AP Photo/Matt York; pages 30-31: © Associated Press; pages 32-33: © Getty Images; page 34:
© AFP/Getty Images; page 35: © Associated Press; page 36: © Getty Images; page 37: © AP
Photo/Richard Vogel; page 39: © Getty Images; page 40: © Luke Frazza/AFP/Getty Images;
page 41: © AP Photo/John Duricka; page 42: © Hoang Dinh Nam/AFP/Getty Images; page 43:
© Cynthia Johnson/Time Life Pictures/Getty Images; page 44: © Associated Press; page 45: ©
Terry Ashe/Time Life Pictures/Getty Images; page 46: © AP Photo/Evan Vucci; page 47: © AP
Photo/Dennis Cook; page 48: © Associated Press.

Library of Congress Cataloging-in-Publication Data is available.

ISBN 978-0-448-45110-7   10 9 8 7 6 5 4 3 2 1

JOHN McCAIN
An American Life

By Spencer Williams
with photographs

Grosset & Dunlap

Senator John McCain of Arizona is running for president in the 2008 election. He is the candidate of the Republican Party.

He talks to people all over the country. He talks about the long war in Iraq, the high price of gas, and the problems of people who have lost their jobs.

On November 4th, he hopes that more Americans will vote for him than for his opponent, Senator Barack Obama of Illinois. Barack Obama is a Democrat. He is also the first black candidate for president.

John McCain

   John McCain has been in the Senate since 1987—that's a long time. Yet he has not spent his whole life in politics. For twenty-two years he was in the military. The men in the McCain family have a long history of serving in the United States Navy.

Both his father and grandfather were four-star admirals. That is the highest rank in the navy. Here the young John McCain (on the left) is with his parents. They are at McCain Field, a U.S. Navy training base named in honor of his grandfather. A framed photo of his grandfather appears at the top of the picture.

John McCain (left) with his father

John McCain might have become an admiral, too. But at age forty-four, he set forth in a new direction—politics.

John McCain was born on August 29, 1936, in the Panama Canal Zone where his father was stationed. Here his grandfather holds baby John. His older sister Sandy is at the left. His younger brother Joseph was born in 1942.

Because of his job in the navy, John's
father was often away. John's mother
Roberta raised the children. She is
ninety-six years old now and very active
in her son's campaign for president.

The McCain family lived all over the United States. John went to about twenty different schools! He was smart—that was for sure. He loved history and literature.

His mother remembers him as a very well-behaved little boy. But by the time he was in high school, he had become a little bit of a rebel. He also had a sharp tongue. At the all-boys prep school in Virginia that he attended, one of his nicknames was McNasty.

Like his father and grandfather, John McCain graduated from the Naval Academy in Annapolis, Maryland. It trains future officers and has many famous graduates including former President Jimmy Carter. After graduation, McCain wanted to fly planes. He spent more than two years training to be a pilot.

McCain had several dangerous mishaps. One plane crashed into a bay off the coast of Texas. Another collided with phone wires in Spain. But McCain was very lucky—he was never seriously hurt.

At an aviation museum, McCain gave a speech in front of an A-4 Skyhawk fighter jet like the one he piloted in Vietnam.

Then in 1966 he
asked to go fight in
Vietnam.

Would his luck
hold?

Why was the United States sending troops to fight a war in Southeast Asia?

After World War II, the United States and the Soviet Union became enemies. The Soviet Union (or Russia) was a huge nation spreading over Europe and Asia.

It was not a democracy with free elections or free speech. It was a communist country. The United States wanted to stop the Russians from taking control of other countries and becoming the strongest superpower in the world.

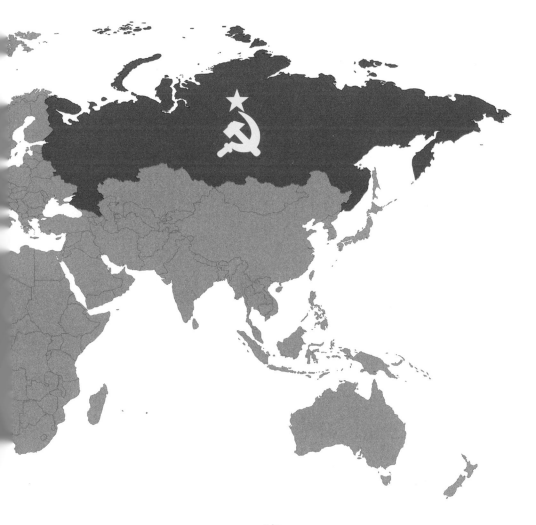

The small, beautiful country of Vietnam is in Southeast Asia. At that time, most of its people were poor rice farmers.

Vietnam was divided into two parts—
North Vietnam and South Vietnam.
North Vietnam was communist and sided
with the Soviet Union. Its leader wanted
to take over South Vietnam so that there
would be one Vietnam, loyal to the Soviet
Union.

The United States wanted to make sure
that didn't happen. By the early 1960s,
the United States was sending troops to
help South Vietnam fight against North
Vietnam.

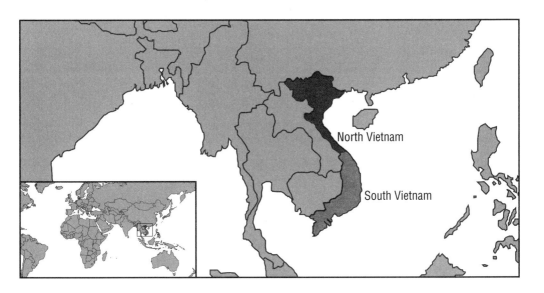

North Vietnam

South Vietnam

In this war, big armies did not fight on open battlefields. The soldiers of North Vietnam staged small, surprise attacks.

Often they attacked in the jungle where it was easy to remain hidden. Often they weren't in uniform. For American troops, it was very hard to tell who were enemies and who were innocent villagers.

Many Americans thought it was wrong for U.S. troops to be in Vietnam. There were many protests against the war. Many soldiers who returned from the war also wanted the fighting to end.

The anti-war movement grew stronger as more and more American soldiers died in Vietnam. There were even protests across the street from the White House.

Still, President Lyndon Johnson would not bring the troops home. He said that he was sure the United States would win in the end. South Vietnam would not fall to Communism. He was wrong. The United States lost the war—it was the first war our country had ever lost. Today Vietnam is no longer divided into two parts. It is one country and it is communist. It also is no longer our enemy.

By the time the war ended, about fifty-eight thousand U.S. soldiers had been killed in Vietnam. A monument in Washington, D.C., honors the Americans who lost their lives there.

It was a sad time for the country. There was a draft—young men over eighteen could be forced to enlist in the military. Many who were against the war found ways to avoid the draft. Some moved to Canada; some went to prison rather than fight in a war they didn't believe in.

John McCain volunteered for combat duty in Vietnam. It must have been a hard decision. The young naval officer had a family now. His wife Carol had been married before. She had two young sons, Douglas and Andrew. John McCain had adopted the boys. The McCains also had a baby daughter, Sidney. They were all living in Florida. However, in 1966, he left for Vietnam. He did not see his family again until 1973.

As a war pilot, McCain would take off in a plane from a giant aircraft carrier. He would drop bombs over enemy areas. Then he would return to the carrier.

One of the carriers that he served on was the USS *Forrestal*.

In July of 1967, the *Forrestal* caught fire. One hundred thirty-four men died onboard the ship. Once again John McCain was lucky. He wasn't hurt. He continued to fly on bombing missions over North Vietnam.

Then, on October 26, 1967, during his twenty-third mission, his plane was shot down over Hanoi, the capital of North Vietnam.

The crash broke both of his arms and one of his legs. He was dragged from the water and beaten by an angry mob. Then he was taken to prison.

John McCain

His captors soon discovered that
McCain's father was a powerful admiral.
John McCain could have won release from
prison quickly. His captors offered him his
freedom many times. He always said no.
What was his reason? Other U.S. soldiers
had been prisoners of war in Vietnam
for a long time. He thought that they
deserved to be freed before he was.

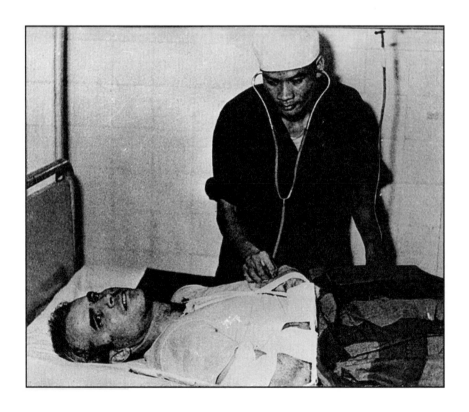

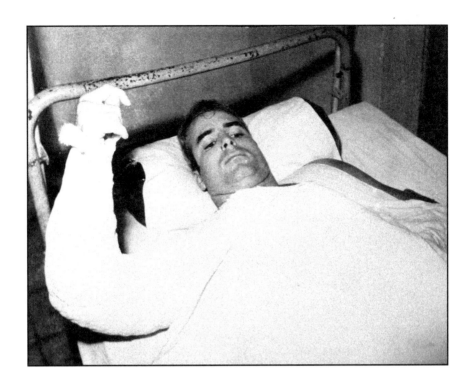

John McCain ended up spending five-and-a-half years in various prisons. At first his captors treated him decently. But after his refusal to leave, that changed. One of the worst prisons was known as the "Hanoi Hilton." American prisoners of war called it that as a joke. It was not at all like a hotel. As John McCain found out, life for a prisoner of war in Vietnam was hardly life at all.

For two years, McCain was kept alone in a cell, away from all the prisoners. He had no contact with anyone except guards. They beat him and tortured him. Yet they never broke his spirit.

This is the front entrance of the "Hanoi Hilton." Many years after he was freed, John McCain took one of his sons to Vietnam and they visited the prison. McCain says that he does not bear ill will toward the people of Vietnam. Yet he finds it hard to forgive his guards.

John McCain came home a war hero in March 1973, soon after the cease-fire in the Vietnam war.

The world had changed while he was a prisoner of war. Richard Nixon was now president. The civil rights movement and the women's movement were powerful forces in American life. Both Martin Luther King Jr. and Robert F. Kennedy had been shot and killed. American astronauts had landed on the moon.

McCain's family had changed, too. His wife Carol had been in a terrible car accident. Both her legs had been shattered. She was still recovering from her injuries. His children were almost six years older.

John McCain with President Richard Nixon

The National War College

John McCain lost no time in picking
up his life. He could no longer fly planes
because of his injuries. He was still in the
navy, though, and he decided to attend the
National War College in Washington, D.C.

He began working with members of the Senate and the House of Representatives. It was McCain's job to explain to Congress what the navy needed to do to remain strong.

It was the beginning of a new chapter in his life. McCain realized he wanted to be in government himself.

He and Carol had gotten divorced. McCain was now married to Cindy Hensley. She was from Arizona. That is where the couple made their home. That is where he began his first campaign.

In 1982, he ran for Congress and won. It was the start of an amazing political career. After two terms in the House of Representatives, McCain ran for the Senate in 1986. He won and has served there ever since.

John McCain with President George H.W. Bush

It was the start of a second family, too. John and Cindy McCain have four children—Jack, Jimmy, Meghan, and Bridget. The McCains adopted Bridget, who was born in Bangladesh.

McCain is respected and popular with voters. He has fought for the rights of Native Americans. He has put forward laws to reform the way politicians raise money for campaigns.

However, in 1988, he and four other senators were accused of giving favors to a banker named Charles Keating. The senators became known as "the Keating Five." In the end, John McCain was not charged with a crime. Still, a special Senate committee said he had used poor judgment.

In 2000, McCain tried to run for president. But George W. Bush became the Republican candidate. Bush has served as president for the past eight years. Now John McCain is the choice of the Republican party. Now he is getting his shot at becoming president.

He is seventy-two years old. Barack Obama is forty-seven. The two men disagree on many things. For instance, John McCain wants the United States to stay in Iraq and win the war there. Barack Obama does not believe our country should have started the war. He wants to start bringing the troops home. Each one thinks he is the best person to lead our country.

Who is right? Only the voters can decide that. And they will—on November 4th.